# MYTHS UNDERSTOOD

# UNDERSTANDING NORSE MYTHS

BRIAN WILLIAMS

Crabtree Publishing Company
www.crabtreebooks.com

Dedicated by Margaret Salter
To Krista Cagg and her Lady Freyja—for the wealth of knowledge they have shared.

**Author:** Brian Williams
**Publishing plan research and development:**
  Sean Charlebois, Reagan Miller
  Crabtree Publishing Company
**Editor-in-chief:** Lionel Bender
**Editors:** Simon Adams, Lynn Peppas
**Proofreaders:** Laura Booth, Wendy Scavuzzo
**Project coordinator:** Kathy Middleton
**Photo research:** Kim Richardson
**Designer:** Ben White
**Cover design:** Margaret Amy Salter
**Production coordinator and Prepress technician:**
  Samara Parent
**Production:** Kim Richardson
**Print coordinator:** Katherine Berti

**Consultants:** Amy Leggett-Caldera, M.Ed., Elementary and Middle School Education Consultant, Mississippi State University.

**Cover:** Yggdrasil, also known as the World Tree (top center and bottom background); raven (top right); Sognefjord, Norway (top left); Jörmungandr, also known as the World Serpent (bottom left); Thor, the God of Thunder (bottom right); Rainbow Bridge of Bifrost (middle center); Viking runestone (bottom center).

**Title page:** Urnes Church carvings

**Photographs and reproductions:**
Cover: Wikimedia Commons: Emil Doepler: bottom left, Arthur Rackham: bottom right; Thinkstock: top and bottom background; Shutterstock: bottom center
Maps: Stefan Chabluk
Interior: ©Mary Evans Picture Library / The Image Works: 8
shutterstock.com: 1 (SOMATUSCAN), 4 (Alfio Ferlito), 4–5 (Irina Afonskaya), 6t (Kachalkina Veronika), 6b (Oleg_Mit), 7 (Santi Rodriguez), 8–9 (Gislij20), 10 (David Persson), 16t (Route66), 16–17 (MP cz), 20–21 (irabel8), 22–23 (corepics), 24 (brandonht), 25t (Route66), 25 (Conny Sjostrom), 26–27 (TTphoto), 32–33 (J. Helgason), 34t (Kachalkina Veronika), 34–35 (tovovan/Shutterstock.com), 40 (SOMATUSCAN), 42 (Ferenc Szelepcsenyi/Shutterstock.com), 44t (Mike Heywood), 44l (immelstorm)
Topfoto: (ARPL/HIP): 30; (British Library Board/Robana ): 41l; (Fortean/Topfoto): 14–15; (The Granger Collection): 13, 18, 21, 26, 29, 37; (Mander and Mitchenson University of Bristol/ArenaPAL): 31; (Roger-Viollet): 39; (Stapleton Historical Collection/Heritage-Images): 5, 11, 23; (Topfoto): 12, 41r; (Topham/PA): 42–43; (Topham Picturepoint): 17; (World History Archive): 35r
Werner Forman Archive: 15 (Universitetets Oldsaksamling, Oslo), 19 (Statens Historiska Museum, Stockholm), 24r (Statens Historiska Museum, Stockholm), 28t (Statens Historiska Museum, Stockholm), 33 (Viking Ship Museum, Bygdoy), 36 (Universitetets Oldsaksamling, Oslo), 38 (Statens Historiska Museum, Stockholm), 44r (Thjodminjasafn, Reykjavik, Iceland National Museum)

This book was produced for Crabtree Publishing Company by Bender Richardson White

**Library and Archives Canada Cataloguing in Publication**

Williams, Brian, 1943-
    Understanding Norse myths / Brian Williams.

(Myths understood)
Includes index.
Issued also in electronic formats.
ISBN 978-0-7787-4527-3 (bound).--ISBN 978-0-7787-4532-7 (pbk.)

    1. Mythology, Norse--Juvenile literature. 2. Scandinavia--Religion--Juvenile literature. I. Title. II. Series: Myths understood

BL860.W55 2012        j293'.13        C2012-906377-0

**Library of Congress Cataloging-in-Publication Data**

CIP available at Library of Congress

# Crabtree Publishing Company

www.crabtreebooks.com        1-800-387-7650

Printed in the U.S.A./112012/FA20121012

**Published in Canada**
**Crabtree Publishing**
616 Welland Ave.
St. Catharines, Ontario
L2M 5V6

**Published in the United States**
**Crabtree Publishing**
PMB 59051
350 Fifth Avenue, 59th Floor
New York, New York 10118

**Published in the United Kingdom**
**Crabtree Publishing**
Maritime House
Basin Road North, Hove
BN41 1WR

**Published in Australia**
**Crabtree Publishing**
3 Charles Street
Coburg North
VIC 3058

# CONTENTS

**WHAT ARE MYTHS?** ................................. 4

What are myths and how have the Norse myths come down to us today? What do the Norse myths explain and what thrilling stories do they tell?

**VIKING SCANDINAVIA** .............................. 6

Where the Vikings came from, how far they traveled, and how their harsh landscape shaped their myths. The Viking myth of how the world was created.

**RELIGION AND GODS** ............................... 10

The many gods and goddesses in Norse myths: who they all are and what forces they control. How the gods quarrel and fight one another.

**THE NATURAL WORLD** ............................. 16

How the Norse myths explain the workings of the natural world such as the melting of the winter ice, the tides, and earthquakes.

**DAILY LIFE** ....................................... 24

Family life, the changing seasons, and other aspects of daily life in Norse times, and how the different myths made sense of it.

**INTO BATTLE** ..................................... 34

Viking raids and battles, and the weapons the Vikings used to overwhelm their opponents. The myth of Ragnarok, the battle at the end of the world.

**NORSE LEGACY** .................................... 40

How Norse culture, myths, and beliefs remain alive today in books, movies, games, and music. Modern words and place names that have Norse origins.

Time Chart      45

Glossary      46

Learning More      47

Index      48

# WHAT ARE MYTHS?

**Myths are stories passed down through many generations. Such stories were told from memory long before people first wrote them down. For the Norse people of Northern Europe, myths explained how the world was made and answered important questions about life and death.**

The Norse people are often known as Vikings. Gods played an important part in Norse myths, along with other **supernatural** beings, although little about the **religion** of the Norse people is actually known. When the Norse peoples of Scandinavia became Christians about 1,000 years ago, their **pagan** temples were destroyed or turned into churches. Old beliefs in ancient gods clung on in myths that passed into literature. **Migrant** Vikings, and **Anglo-Saxons** from Germany who shared the same myths, took the old tales to new lands.

Norse myths were thrilling stories about gods, heroes, giants, **dwarves,** wild animals, and fierce monsters. Like myths in other cultures, Norse myths include creation stories that explain how the world

## THE EDDAS

The *Eddas* from medieval Iceland are the main written sources for Norse myths. The *Poetic Edda,* or *Elder Edda,* is a collection of 38 poems made between 1000 and 1200 C.E. It tells of heroes such as Sigurd and of the beginning and ending of the world. The *Prose Edda,* or *Younger Edda,* was written down in about 1270 by Snorri Sturluson as a guide for poets, in which he used numerous Norse myths as examples.

came into existence. They explain natural **phenomena** such as the crack of thunder and the tremor of an earthquake.

The myths were first told aloud as stories and poems. They were sung in the halls and palaces of kings and were a way of passing on history, legend, fact, and fiction. The myths were not written down until the Viking age was almost over. Some were recorded by unknown authors, others by an Icelander named Snorri Sturlusson.

*Right:* In this 1924 illustration of a Norse myth, the beautiful Grimhilde, mother of the warrior Hagen, is courted by the ugly dwarf Alberich.

*Left:* Viking history is still celebrated every year in Russia during Moscow's City Day.

5

# VIKING SCANDINAVIA

**The Norse people lived in Scandinavia, which included modern-day Sweden, Norway, Finland, and Denmark. Their myths and some gods were shared by Germanic peoples to their south, such as the Anglo-Saxons. The rugged northern landscape made these stories.**

Europe's northlands are regions of forests, mountains, lakes, and glaciers. In the short months of summer sun, meadows fill with bright wildflowers, crops ripen, and farm animals graze. Winter brings short days and long, cold nights of darkness. The climate is as harsh as the craggy landscape, with plenty of freezing fog, hail, rain, and snow. Winter ice freezes the rivers and tidal inlets. Storms lash the land and sea with thunder and lightning.

The roots of Norse myths lay in the mountains and forests of these northlands, among small **isolated** communities ruled by warrior-kings. Most people were farmers, seafarers, and traders, who took their tales of gods, goddesses, heroes, and monsters wherever they roamed. The stories were about the often violent world of the Norse gods.

## THE NINE WORLDS

**Muspelheim**—land of fire

**Alfheim**—home of the elves, or light elves

**Vanaheim**—home of the Vanir gods

**Asgard**—home of the Aesir gods

**Midgard**—home of humans

**Jotunheim**—home of the giants

**Svartalfheim**—home of the dwarves, or dark elves

**Helheim**—land of the dead

**Niflheim**—world of ice and mist

*Above:* The island of Magerøya in the extreme north of Norway has a typical Norse landscape.

NORTH
AMERICA

GREENLAND

ICELAND

VINLAND

N

SCANDINAVIA

~ Viking routes

Viking territory

500 Miles

500 Kilometers

RUSSIA

BRITAIN

GERMANY

FRANCE

SPAIN

GREECE    TURKEY

*Left:* This statue in Reykjavik, Iceland, is of Leif Eriksson (Leifur Eiriksson), an explorer regarded as the first European to land in North America.

*Above:* This map shows how far the Vikings roamed from their homelands, traveling by sea to Iceland, Greenland, and North America, and by land and river across Europe into Asia.

## THEMES IN NORSE MYTHS

Hardship and danger were popular themes in Norse myths, as were wars between the gods and their enemies. **Odin**, god of warriors, welcomes dead warriors to **Valhalla**. There is feasting and laughter, but in the Norse world there is also trickery and treachery. Fate can raise a person high, then dash them to destruction. Often things are not what they seem. What matters are loyalty, kinship, beauty, fertility, courage, and endurance. The myth of the frost giant Ymir explains how this strange, dangerous world was made.

### GIANT MYTHS

Many myths have stories of giants, and creation stories that tell how the world was made. In Greek myth, Gaia (Earth) gave birth to a race of giants called Titans. The Inuit people of North America told how, in the beginning, there were a pair of giants whose daughter Sedna grew even bigger than her parents. Giants were a way to explain gigantic natural forces such as geysers, glaciers, icebergs, mountains, and rocks.

*Below:* The giant Ymir was the first living being in Scandinavian mythology. He was created from melting ice and was fed by the cow Audhumbla.

*Right:* Hot steam, mud, and water spouts from a Scandinavian **geyser**, as in the fiery southern world of Muspelheim.

# HOW THE WORLD WAS MADE

In the beginning, there were the lands of fire and ice. Fiery Muspelheim was a southern world of bright warmth and light. Between it and the icy north stretched the void of Ginnungagap.

In this void, where heat and cold met, a giant named Ymir formed from the ice-melt. From his left arm grew the first man and woman. From his legs came the family of frost giants. Ymir drank milk from a cow. As the cow licked at the salty ic,e she freed a man named Buri.

Buri's son Bor fathered the gods Odin, Vili, and Ve. These gods then killed Ymir, and all the frost giants drowned in his blood, except one named Bergelmir.

From Ymir's body the world was formed. From his blood came the sea and lakes, and his flesh formed the land. His bones made the mountains. Rocks and pebbles came from his teeth, jaws, and broken bones. The giant's skull formed the arching sky, with a dwarf at each corner to hold it high above Earth. This was the world of men, Midgard, or Middle Earth, with Ymir's eyebrows creating a wall to protect it.

To fill this world with people, the gods turned two trees on the seashore into a man and a woman. They made the dwarves, skilled craftsmen of the land, hills, and rocks. Time was created. Night and Day drove **chariots** across the sky. Girl-Sun and Boy-moon were chased across the sky by wolves. If the great wolf swallowed the Sun, all things would end.

# RELIGION *AND* GODS

## THE WEAVING OF FATE

The fate of men and women in Midgard was determined, not by the gods, but by the three Norns. These three are much like the witches who foresee the future in Shakespeare's play *Macbeth*.

At the Well of Urd, the gods went to settle arguments and seek advice from the Norns—three sisters who sat spinning the thread of fate. A broken thread meant the end of a life. The three Norns were Urd (the past), Verdandi (the present), and Skuld (the future). Urd and Verdandi were kindly sisters, but Skuld often tore their work to shreds.

The Norns refreshed the tree Yggdrasil from the well, sprinkling dew upon Earth. The sisters were said to visit Earth as swans, giving advice to **mortals**.

**Norse gods fought monsters and giants. Yet even the gods would die in battle, when a new world would emerge. People believed in life after death, either in Hel (the underworld) or in Valhalla (Odin's hall).**

At the heart of the Norse world was Yggdrasil, the World Tree. Its roots reached three ways, into the lands of the Aesir, the giants, and the dead. Around the Aesir gods' stronghold of **Asgard**, and the human world of Midgard or Middle Earth, stretched an ocean. The worlds were linked by a rainbow bridge—Bifrost—guarded by the god Heimdall, whose horn blasts rang across the worlds.

Odin, king of the Aesir, was also known as Woden or Wotan. He was the master of magic, god of poetry and battles, and restored the dead to life. He drank from the spring of Mimir to gain wisdom and understanding, but paid the price of an eye to do so, so he was Odin the one-eyed.

*Right:* The three Norns, all daughters of Erda, the goddess of wisdom and Earth, were spinners of the thread of fate that could end a life.

## THE NORSE GODS

The chief Norse gods, led by Odin, were

**Thor**—thunder god, eldest son of Odin

**Baldur**—son of Odin, fairest of all

**Tyr**—giver of victory in battle

**Bragi**—skilled in words and poetry

**Heimdall**—guardian of the gods

**Loki**—son of a giant, a cunning schemer

**Ull**—famous archer and skier

**Forseti**—son of Baldur, the lawgiver

**Hoder**—a blind god, twin of Baldur

**Hermod**—brother of Baldur

**Hoenir**—companion to Odin and Loki in their wanderings

**Njord**—Vanir god who controlled the winds and sea

**Freyr**—son of Njord, giver of sunshine, rain, peace, and plenty

# ODIN'S MAGICAL HORSE

Odin's ravens, Hugin (thought) and Munin (memory), flew through the world and told him of its doings. By flinging his magic spear, Odin caused war on Earth. His horse Sleipnir was faster than any other. This story illustrates the cunning of Loki, as well as the Norse admiration for fine horses.

One day, a giant offered to build a wall around Asgard. Odin agreed. If the giant finished the work in one winter, the giant would win the goddess Freyja, the Sun, and the Moon. If not, he would lose his life. The gods thought the task impossible, but the giant had a marvelous horse, Svadilfari, who moved huge stones by night. Before spring, the work was almost done. The gods turned to Loki for advice. Turning himself into a beautiful mare, Loki lured the stallion Svadilfari away. The wall was unfinished and the giant was killed. Svadilfari's colt, the eight-legged Sleipnir, became Odin's horse, the swiftest of steeds.

**Below:** On this Viking picture stone, Odin is shown entering Valhalla riding the eight-legged Sleipnir.

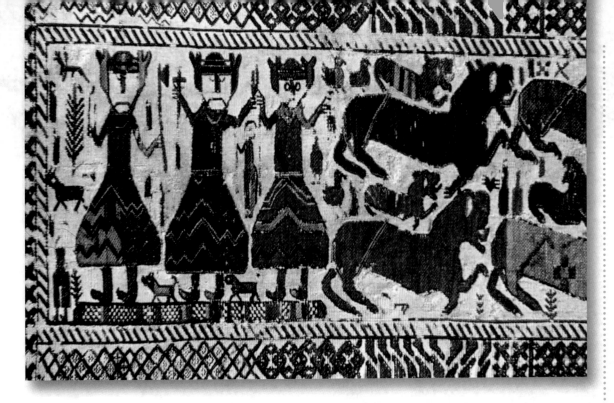

*Above:* On this Swedish wall hanging from the late 1100s, Thor, Odin, and Frigg are shown with animals in a farming scene.

## FAMILIES OF GODS

The Aesir gods lived as a rather quarrelsome family, keeping watch from Asgard's halls and palaces, just as Norse villagers always kept a lookout for their many enemies. Sharing the land and oceans with humans were the Vanir gods—a less violent family.

Odin and his wife Frigg had several sons. People especially loved Thor, who was bold and hot tempered. He protected farms, homes, and ships at sea. Odin and his family often turned to Loki for help. Loki was the son of fire giants.

Odin's blood brother, Loki, was an entertaining joker who was untrustworthy. Loki's cunning later turned to evil. He caused the death of Odin's son, Baldur the fair, who was the most-loved god of all.

### THE NORSE GODDESSES

Chief among the Asgard women were
**Frigg**—wife of Odin, who shared his knowledge of the future
**Freyja**, twin sister of Freyr—helped in love affairs
**Skadi**—wife of Njord the sea god, hunted in the mountains
**Idun**—wife of Bragi, guarded the apples of immortality that kept the gods young
**Sif**—wife of Thor, with beautiful golden hair
**Nanna**—wife of Baldur
**Sigyn**—wife of Loki
**Gna** and **Fulla**—servants of Frigg
**Gefion**—received unmarried girls after death
**Gerda**—beloved by Freyr

## MONSTERS, GIANTS, AND MAGIC

Supernatural beings were part of Norse myth. Giants waged war with the gods, and ugly slow-witted **trolls** lay in wait in the mountains. Fierce **dragons** guarded treasure-hoards and foul monsters stalked the lakes and mountains. The wolves Skoll and Hati pursued the Sun and Moon. When they almost swallowed their prey, people witnessed a solar or lunar eclipse. This myth explained such alarming natural phenomena.

Many stories involved shape-changing. Odin could become an animal, but often roamed Earth like a wizard in a cloak and wide-brimmed hat. There was magic everywhere. Dwarves guarded magic rings in dark caves. The gods often seemed like witches moving about the sky, such as Freyja in her chariot pulled by cats. As this next myth reveals, an otter might be a man and even a gold ring could bring misfortune.

### MODERN TROLLS

A few wolves still live in Scandinavia but no real-life animal resembles the troll of myths. Trolls were always unpleasant. The term "troll" now describes someone who posts nasty messages on the Internet.

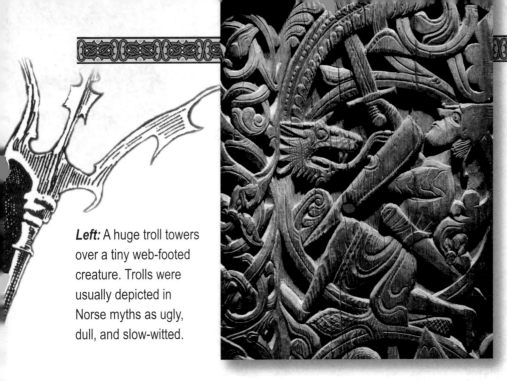

**Left:** In this wooden carving from a church doorway, Sigurd kills the dragon Fafnir.

**Left:** A huge troll towers over a tiny web-footed creature. Trolls were usually depicted in Norse myths as ugly, dull, and slow-witted.

## THE RING AND THE DRAGON

**The dwarves or dark elves forged wondrous swords and golden treasures for the gods. This myth reveals the Norse fascination with gold, magic rings, shape-changing, revenge, and curses.**

Challenged by Loki, the dwarves made three wonderful objects: a boar with golden bristles that could light the darkest night; the gold ring Draupnir, which made more gold rings; and Mjölnir, the hammer that hit whatever it was thrown at before returning to the thrower.

One day, Loki and Odin saw an otter. Loki killed the otter, but it was really a man in animal shape. As payment for his death, the dead man's family demanded the otter skin be filled to overflowing with gold. The skin kept stretching, however. So Loki sought out the dwarf-king Andvari, who was hiding in the form of a fish, and demanded his treasure. The dwarf held onto one gold ring, which was the magic ring Draupnir. The ring had the power to make him rich again. Loki grabbed the ring and hauled it away with the rest of the treasure. However, Andvari had put a curse on the ring that would destroy any new owner. The curse of the ring came to pass. After the otter skin was covered with gold, the sons killed their father. One son, Fafnir, changed into a dragon to guard the gold. He was slain by the hero Sigurd.

# THE NATURAL WORLD

**A good harvest was vital if families were to survive the long winter. People looked to kindly gods, such as Baldur, Sif, and the twins Freyr and Freyja, to bring them good harvests.**

Norse farmers grew crops of oats, barley, and rye, and vegetables such as onions, beans, and cabbages. They raised cattle, sheep, goats, pigs, and chickens. Farming families marked the changing seasons with festivals. The story of Baldur was a poetic way to explain the fading of the light, as the brief northern summer gave way to the long dark winter.

*Below:* Some Viking chiefs lived in large halls like this modern reconstruction in Norway, but most people lived in smaller wooden huts.

# THE DEATH OF BALDUR

**Odin and Frigg had twin sons. Baldur was god of beauty, goodness, and light. His brother Hoder was the blind god of darkness. This myth refers to plants and life.**

Gentle Baldur was loved by all. The Sun seemed to shine from him. He lived in a hall in Asgard called Breidablik with his wife Nanna (blossom). Baldur knew the magic of **runes** and healing but he did not know his own fate. When his brightness dimmed, his parents asked him what was wrong. Baldur confessed that troubling dreams made him afraid. Odin and Frigg were fearful, so Frigg begged all things on Earth to promise they would never hurt Baldur. All agreed. But one tiny plant—the mistletoe—was overlooked.

   The gods enjoyed sports, especially throwing things. One day, they tried a new game. Knowing that nothing could hurt Baldur, they threw all sorts of things at him, laughing as the objects swerved from their target. However, Loki was jealous of Baldur's unmatched brightness and saw a chance to be rid of him. Disguised as an old woman, Loki found out from Frigg that the mistletoe alone had not agreed to keep Baldur safe.

   Loki made a spear from the mistletoe plant and gave it to blind Hoder, offering to help him play the new game. Guided by Loki, Hoder threw the spear and Baldur fell dead. To save Baldur from Hel, all things on Earth were asked to weep for him. All did, except for a giantess in a cave, said to be Loki in disguise.

***Right:*** Loki—sometimes a god, sometimes a giant—was a trickster and thief in Norse myth. He caused the death of Baldur at the hands of the blind god Hoder. Loki gave Hoder a mistletoe spear and helped him throw it so it would kill Baldur.

## ANIMALS AND TREES

People told many stories about the animals and trees that shared their world. Most important was the World Tree, Yggdrasil, forever at risk from creatures that preyed upon it. It was an ash tree, with an eagle at its top and a coiling dragon-snake named Nidhog, who gnawed at the roots of the tree, trying to kill it. The eagle and serpent were enemies and traded insults through a

*Above:* People caring for Yggdrasil, the World Tree. The tree was often in danger from creatures that attacked it, notably the snake that gnawed at the roots, and the deer and goats that nibbled at its leaves.

squirrel-messenger named Ratatosk. Deer and goats nibbled the leaves of the tree.

Forest trees had magical importance in Norse myths. Old Norse pagan temples were probably made from giant trees, and people made **sacrifices** to the gods in forest groves. Christian missionaries cut down sacred trees but built wooden churches that from the outside probably looked much like the old Norse temples.

The wolf was a predator feared by farmers but also admired for its strength. In Norse myth, Fenrir, father of wolves, was fated to kill Odin at the end of the world. The wolf is often the villain in myths, as it is in the fairy tale of Little Red Riding Hood. But no wolf was as terrible as Fenrir, as the story of his binding made clear.

**Above:** Tyr, who is the giver of victory in battle, is shown on the left with the chained Fenrir, whom Tyr guarded at the cost of his own hand.

## THE BINDING OF FENRIR

**Loki married the giantess Angrboda and had three monster-children. They were Hel ,"goddess of the dead;" Jormungand, the "World Serpent;" and the wolf Fenrir.**

Fenrir was reared in Asgard, where only Tyr was brave enough to feed him. The gods kept Fenrir chained, because the Norns had warned that the great wolf would one day kill Odin. They asked the dwarves to forge an unbreakable chain and from the roots of a mountain, the sound of a cat's footsteps, and the breath of a fish, the dwarves made a silk-like ribbon.

The gods asked Fenrir if they could tie him up to test the cord's strength. Though suspicious, Fenrir agreed, providing one of the gods put a hand in his jaws while the binding was done. Tyr agreed. When Fenrir found himself trapped, he bit off the god's hand. Fenrir was kept bound until the last day of Ragnarok, when he would break free to take revenge.

## THOR GOES FISHING

Thor was the thunder god and was known for his strength. He was Odin's first son. His mother was an Earth-giant. Thor had three special treasures: Mjölnir, the hammer that could shatter rock and slay giants; a belt to double his strength; and iron gloves to grasp Mjölnir.

Thor went fishing with the giant Hymir, taking the head of the giant's biggest ox for bait. Thor rowed way out into the ocean and threw the head overboard. Hymir panicked when the fearsome World Serpent, Jormungand, reared up to snatch the ox-head. Using all his strength, Thor pushed through the bottom of the boat into the sea. He dragged up the monster and raised his hammer to strike, but at that moment the giant cut the fishing line. The serpent sank back into the depths. Enraged, Thor knocked the giant overboard and waded ashore.

Hymir returned home with two whales for breakfast, then challenged Thor to break his drinking cup. The cup would not break, until Thor was told to fling it at the giant's head. The cup shattered into fragments, which caused the melting ice to crack and freed the Arctic Ocean.

*Right:* The stormy seas around the coasts of Scandinavia are the setting for many favorite Norse myths.

## THOR AND THE TIDES

In a drinking contest with giants, Thor was tricked. Trying to empty a drinking horn, he found that the horn's mouth lay in the ocean, so he was swallowing sea water. His gulps caused the ocean to ebb to low tide.

## THOR AND THE SEA

Myths helped to explain the geography of the Norse lands and especially the ocean, which featured in many stories. Njord the sea god dwelt on land but lived close to the sea, just as many Vikings did in their villages along the coast. Another important sea god, Aegir, lived beneath the waves in a palace full of treasure from lost ships.

Thor and the other gods liked to visit Aegir, king of the sea creatures, to drink his fine beer and **mead**. Myths explained the tides, which were caused when Thor tried to drink the ocean; and thunderstorms, which were caused when Thor fought a giant serpent. By smashing a giant's drinking cup, Thor brought about the summer break-up of the Arctic ice, as told in the myth of Thor's fishing.

*Left:* In the myth about Thor's fishing expedition with Hymir, Thor quarreled with Hymir and knocked the giant out of the boat.

## HOW LOKI CAUSED EARTHQUAKES

**Earthquakes and volcanoes, common in Iceland, may have colored the story of Ragnarok—the battle at the end of the world. Loki was responsible for earthquakes.**

Loki was at first the spirit of hearth fire and life. He loved mischief and trickery. The gods relied on his cunning to get them out of trouble. But Loki gradually turned into a selfish and evil figure. After causing Baldur's death, Loki killed a servant at a feast in Asgard, then shouted insults at the gods. He became an **outcast**, so he hid in the mountains. When Odin and Thor came after him, Loki turned himself into a salmon and jumped into a waterfall. The gods netted him and bound him in iron. The giantess Skadi placed a serpent above him, letting its poison drop onto Loki's face. Loki's wife Sigyn stayed beside him, catching the poison in a cup. Only when the cup was full did she move to empty it. The poison hit Loki's face again. His struggles to get free caused the land to shudder with earthquakes.

*Right:* In Norse myth, Gerda was the spirit of the Aurora Borealis or Northern Lights.

## WILD LANDSCAPE

The northern landscape with its scenery of forests, lakes, mountains, waterfalls, **fjords**, and glaciers formed a natural setting for the dramas of the gods. Rivers were the boundaries between Earth and the underworld and were inhabited by water spirits called nixies. From the clouds above, Thor hurled thunderbolts and lightning flashes in his anger. When storm winds howled, people stayed indoors by their fires, telling tales of the Wild Hunt— unearthly hunters riding across the sky. In the storm clouds, too, they might glimpse the beautiful Valkyries galloping on horses with manes shedding icy hail on the land below. Natural forces, such as storms, volcanoes, and geysers, were so destructive that people thought they must be the work of the gods. One story told how the punishment of Loki, the trickster god who turned evil, caused the ground to tremble.

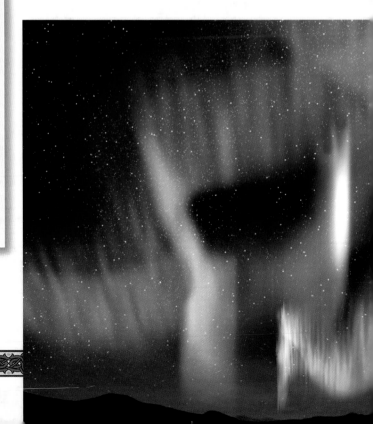

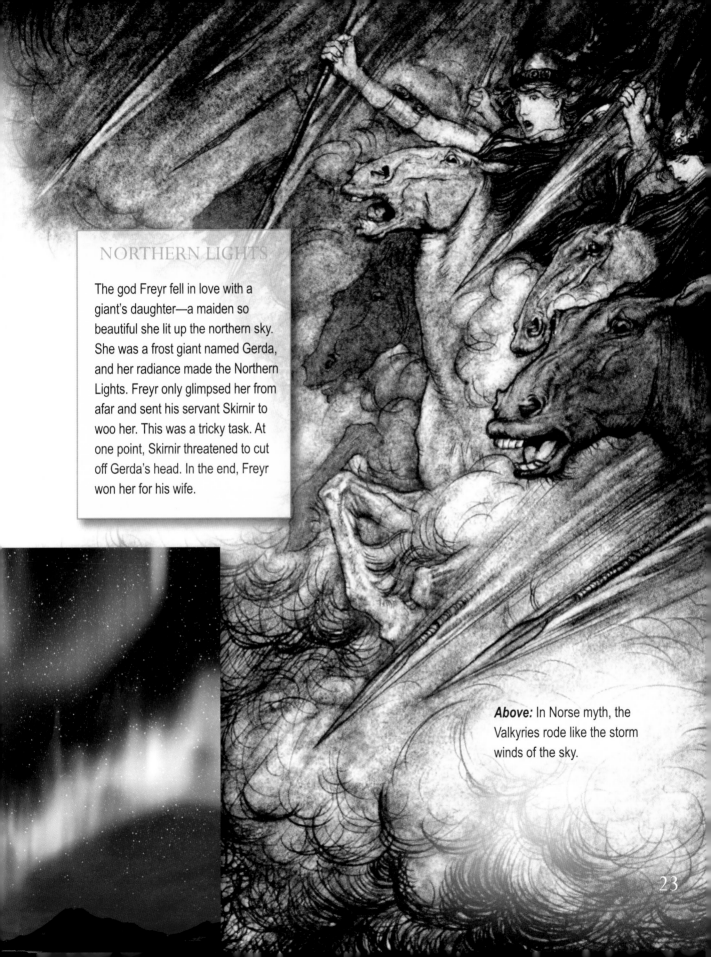

## NORTHERN LIGHTS

The god Freyr fell in love with a giant's daughter—a maiden so beautiful she lit up the northern sky. She was a frost giant named Gerda, and her radiance made the Northern Lights. Freyr only glimpsed her from afar and sent his servant Skirnir to woo her. This was a tricky task. At one point, Skirnir threatened to cut off Gerda's head. In the end, Freyr won her for his wife.

*Above:* In Norse myth, the Valkyries rode like the storm winds of the sky.

23

# DAILY LIFE

Daily life for most people meant the hard toil of a farmer living in a small village or farmstead. For leadership, they looked to their chief or king. Warriors fought for their king as a matter of honor and duty.

*Right:* In this small figure of Odin, his right eye is depicted as a single line, as Odin gave one of his eyes in return for knowledge.

The bonds that held society together were loyalty and gift-giving. Vikings believed that a good warrior must fight bravely for his leader—to the death, if need be. In return, he would be rewarded with gifts and would take his place at table in the great hall. After victory in battle, the king shared treasure with his followers. To be banished from the hall for a crime was to become an outcast.

Viking society seems male dominated, but Viking women had more freedom than women in many other ancient societies. Women could own land and speak alongside men at meetings

## VALHALLA

Odin ruled like a Norse king but his rewards were more than gold. Odin welcomed dead heroes to his hall of Valhalla. Each day, the dead went out to battle, returning in the evening, wounds healed, to feast again. Valhalla became the symbol of a heaven for warriors. In the 1930s and 1940s, German leader Adolf Hitler and his Nazi Party used Norse mythology in their **propaganda**. The Nazis said that German soldiers killed at the battle for Stalingrad in Russia in 1942–1943 had gone to Valhalla.

## LINK TO TODAY

Viking settlers in Iceland in 930 set up the *Althing*, often said to be the world's first **parliament**. Iceland's Althing still makes the nation's laws.

known as *things*, where people gathered to settle disputes and pass laws. Women looked after farms and families when men were away.

Odin ruled as a king in Asgard, but his wife Frigg was clever enough to get Odin to do what she wanted. Odin was not a faithful husband. Like other god-kings—Zeus in Greek myth, for example—he often strayed into love affairs with other goddesses or with human women. Even so, Frigg remained loyal to him.

***Below:*** This Viking coin is a replica of one found in the Thingvellir National Park in Iceland, site of the Althing.

25

## AEGIR AND THE WAVES

Aegir the sea giant was king of the sea creatures. He and his wife Ran had nine daughters. Viking sailors named nine types of ocean waves after the god's daughters.

## THE SEA AND SHIPS

Norse people were bold sailors who built fast sailing vessels called **longships**, each of which could carry 30 warriors. Slower freight ships or *knorrs* carried families and animals. The ships had oars and a sail, and carried people along rivers or over oceans. Viking migrants settled in the Faroe and Shetland Islands, Iceland, and Greenland, to where Erik the Red

*Left:* A replica of the helmet found at Sutton Hoo in England. The original dates to about 625 C.E.

sailed in 985 C.E. Erik's son Leif and other Vikings visited North America about 1000.

Dead kings were sometimes buried in ships, usually on land instead of being set adrift blazing at sea. A ship-burial found in 1939 at Sutton Hoo, England, is thought to be that of King Raedwald, who died about 625. His family probably came from Sweden, so, in Norse tradition, he was buried with his treasure and war gear.

*Below:* The outline of a Viking ship buried underground was marked with upright stones placed on the ground.

## NJORD MARRIES SKADI

**The myth of the sea god Njord and his wife Skadi explained why winter and summer were different. It showed that the Norse liked a joke.**

Njord was the god of winds, sea, and ships and the spirit of good fishing and summer plenty. One day Skadi, daughter of the giant Thjazi, came to Asgard seeking revenge for her father's death at the gods' hands. A winter goddess, she wore silvery armor, a white hunting dress, fur leggings, and snowshoes. The gods angered Skadi by refusing to fight her and offered payment instead. It took all Loki's skill as a joker to make her smile, whereupon the gods offered to let Skadi choose one of them as her husband by looking at their feet. They stood behind a curtain and Skadi gazed at the gods' toes. One pair of beautiful feet stood out, surely the handsome Baldur's? But no, Skadi had picked out Njord. The two were married, but Skadi missed the mountains and complained that the seagulls' cries disturbed her sleep. Njord could not bear to leave the seashore, so winter (Skadi) and summer (Njord) separated. Skadi returned to hunt in the mountains.

**Below:** This pendant represents the goddess Freyja. Around her shoulders is the necklace the dwarves made for her.

## CHANGELINGS

People feared that **elves** or trolls might steal a child, replacing it with one of their own, called a changeling. A child who had a defect or behaved oddly might be suspected of being a changeling.

## FAMILY LIFE

Several generations—children, parents, and grandparents—often shared one house. Men, women, and children worked on the farm or in workshops, where they made goods to use or trade. They all looked after the farm animals and gathered wild berries and nuts. Children helped herd cows and sheep, and kept watch for wolves.

Marriages were often arranged, but a woman could divorce her husband. She was also free to possess her own land and property. Rich Viking chiefs sometimes had two or more wives. Women asked the goddess Freyja for aid in childbirth and for healthy babies. Women raised children, cooked meals, baked bread, and made clothes. An important task was spinning wool into yarn to weave cloth. Men wore cloth pants and a tunic. Women wore a long simple dress with a tunic on top. Leather boots lined with fur kept people's feet warm and dry throughout the cold winter.

**Left:** Elves and fairies play together in an enchanted forest.

## HEIMDALL AND HUMANS

**In Norse society, serfs (slaves) were at the bottom, farmers and others in the middle, and nobles (jarls) at the top. This myth shows how these social orders came about.**

Heimdall stood watch at Bifrost, the rainbow bridge that linked Asgard to Earth. He could hear the sound of things growing, such as grass or wool on a sheep. He could see 100 miles (160 kilometers) away, even at night. Across the bridge he galloped on his horse Gull-top, bringing in the morning. When the frost giants attacked, Heimdall's horn Gjallarhorn sounded to signal the last battle, Ragnarok.

Wandering the land one day, Heimdall found a poor old couple in a hut by the sea. They asked him to share their porridge and he stayed three days. The woman later had a child named Thrall, who was a strong, hard worker. From Thrall came all the serfs and workers of the northlands. Next Heimdall stayed at a farm, where the wife had a boy named Karl, who fathered a race of farmers. Lastly Heimdall stayed at a hilltop castle, where he was offered rich meats and wines. The lady there gave birth to a handsome boy named Jarl, who was a hunter and doer of brave deeds. A line of nobles and the first king of Denmark were descendants of Jarl.

# BRUNHILD

The story of the Valkyrie maiden Brunhild was about magic, like the best fairytales. It is similar to the story of Sleeping Beauty.

Odin's Valkyries rode into battle on flying horses, flourishing spears and directing the fighting on Odin's orders. When not in battle, Valkyries might visit Earth as swans. In a lonely stream, they would fling off their feathers to bathe. If a man stole a Valkyrie's swan **plumage** she could never escape him.

One day, Brunhild and her swan-maiden sisters lost their plumage to a king while bathing. They fell into his power. He demanded that Brunhild give him victory in his next battle and the death of his enemy. But Odin favored the enemy and was furious with Brunhild for going against him. To punish her, he caused her to prick herself on a magic thorn, which made her fall asleep. Then he walled her up in a ring of fire. Brunhild was no longer a Valkyrie but an ordinary human. Only a man brave enough to ride through the flame-wall could rescue and marry her. The hero who did so was Sigurd, or Siegfried.

*Right:* Brunhild pleads for forgiveness from Odin, who has punished her for going against him by walling her up inside a ring of fire from which she cannot escape.

## FRIENDLY DWARVES

The dwarf Gimli in *The Lord of the Rings* is more friendly than some Norse-myth dwarves. Dobby, the kindly house-elf friend of Harry Potter, is a modern version of the old Norse kobold.

*Right:* A theater poster from 1947 advertising a concert of the music to *Snow White and The Seven Dwarfs*.

Harry Benet
(By arrangement with Walt Disney Mickey Mouse Ltd.) presents The only Stage Production of

Walt Disney's Masterpiece
Snow White
and The Seven Dwarfs
with all the original music from the film.

## SNOW WHITE

Dwarves appear in many fairytales, most famously in the story of Snow White, who is helped by seven dwarves.

## FEASTS AND FAIRYTALES

In the king's hall, court poets called *skalds* entertained with songs and stories of gods, goddesses, heroes, monsters, and battles. In battle, a skald's verses could bring victory. Favorite tales at feasts told of dwarves (dark elves) and Valkyries, Odin's fair maidens.

Dwarves were not always friendly creatures. The gods treated them badly, despite the dwarves' great skill as **smiths**. The light elves were more kindly and so usually were *kobolds*. Kobolds were "house-elves" who helped with chores but could also play tricks. They were thanked with offerings of milk.

The Norse people had three main seasonal festivals for feasts and fun: Sigrblot, in early summer, Vetrarblot, the harvest feast, and Jolablot, in mid-winter. They loved sports such as swimming, horse races, rowing, ice skating, and skiing. At feasts, drinkers passed a large cow-horn around the table—the drinking horn could not be set down until empty. They praised the god Odin, who made the "golden mead" Odhaerir, which brought poetry to humans.

*Below:* A herd of free-roaming Icelandic horses shiver in the winter.

## TRADE AND COMMERCE

Norse people traded far from home, gathering at market towns such as Kaupang in Norway, Birka in Sweden, and Hedeby in Denmark. At these centers for trade and **commerce**, merchants traded goods from as far away as Russia and the Middle East. Coins and shells from Arabia and central Asia traveled many miles (kilometers), as far as Viking Jorvik (York) in England, to be found in modern times by **archaeologists.**

## SKILLFUL CRAFTS

Viking trade goods included slaves, dried fish, animal pelts, walrus ivory and hide (made into ropes), deer antlers, duck down feathers, iron, and timber. Vikings went home with jewels, silver, fine silks, wine, and other luxuries. Every Viking settlement had a craft quarter, with people making goods of leather, wood, metal, and ceramics. From these goods, they created everything from swords to boots to coins. The story of Freyr's ship shows how important ships were and, again, how Loki was useful but never to be trusted.

# FREYR'S SHIP

**Freyr, the god who gave sunshine, rain, peace, and plenty, had a marvelous ship made for him by the dwarves.**

This ship, *Skidbladnir*, was big enough to carry the gods and their horses, yet could be folded up and placed in a pocket.

*Below:* This carved wood dragon-head post came from a Viking ship buried at Oseberg around 850 C.E.

Freyr's ship was a gift from Loki, to regain his goodwill after a typical mischievous deed. Thor's wife Sif had wonderful golden hair, like ripe grain in a summer field. But, one morning, she woke to find all her hair shaved off.

At once Sif and Thor suspected Loki. Thor caught the trickster and threatened to kill him, but Loki assured Thor he could restore Sif's hair. Loki made his way to Svartalfaheim to beg the dwarf Dvalin for some golden hair. He also asked for a gift each for Odin and Freyr, who were also angry with him. Dvalin made the hair, which grew on Sif's head as splendidly as her own had done. For Freyr he made *Skidbladnir*, a ship that could sail on water or in the air, and always had favorable winds to fill its sail.

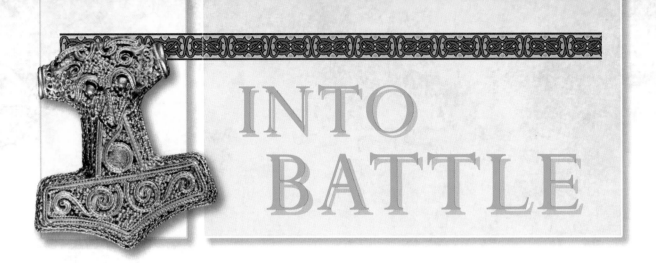

# INTO BATTLE

From the late 700s C. E., Viking raids struck terror into communities along the northern coasts of Europe. Christian churches had a special prayer: "God, deliver us from the fury of the Northmen." As pagans, the early Vikings had no regard for Christian churches or monasteries. Many Vikings were happy to live as peaceful farmers, but they were feared and respected as fierce fighters.

*Below:* Each year, modern Russians dress up in Norse clothing and carry old weapons to celebrate Norse achivements in battle.

Vikings raided in small war bands, although sometimes large armies landed from ships to march inland. Raiders took treasure, cattle, and horses, as well as captives for slaves. Kings fought their neighbors for territory. The strongest kings ruled large regions. One of the most powerful was King Cnut. In the early 1000s, he ruled a Norse empire including England, Norway, and Denmark.

Warriors fought for their king out of loyalty and to earn a place in Valhalla.

To be welcomed into Valhalla was a Viking warrior's reward for loyalty and courage. Vikings fought bravely, believing that if they were killed they would feast with Odin in his hall for heroes. The hall's golden walls were roofed with shields held up by spears. They would feast on food and drink served by the beautiful Valkyries. Valhalla had more than 500 doors, each wide enough for a Viking army to pass through.

LINK TO TODAY

In battle, enemies most feared Viking "berserkers." Clad in bearskins, these Vikings fought without fear or regard for their lives, possibly having taken drugs in the form of magic mushrooms. The expression "to go berserk" is used today for someone who acts in a crazy way.

## WEAPONS

Vikings in battle fought mostly on foot, with swords, spears, and axes. A Viking's sword was a prized possession passed from father to son, and was often inscribed with magic runes to protect the owner. They were made of iron or, in rare cases, steel. Swords and spears were given names—Odin's spear was Gungnir. The Viking battle axe was a favorite weapon, swung with two hands, like Thor's hammer, Mjölnir. Viking warriors wore little armor other than iron helmets. Odin's helmet, however, was made of gold.

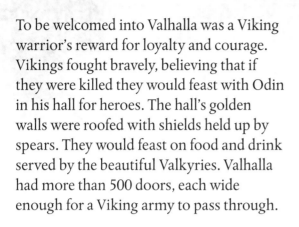

**Right:** Viking warriors wore helmets that had a strip of metal down the front to protect the nose.

## SIGURD THE DRAGONSLAYER

**Sigurd's story is told in a medieval Icelandic poem, the *Volsunga Saga*. He gains the treasure of the Nibelungs and wears a cloak that makes him invisible.**

Sigurd has a magic sword forged by the dwarf-smith Regin. He slays the dragon Fafnir, who guards the golden treasure. Sigurd rescues Brunhild from her fiery prison, but dies from a spear-thrust to the only mortal part of his body: a leaf-sized spot on his back. His story, also told in the German *Nibelungenlied*, inspired later writers, artists, and musicians, including the German composer Richard Wagner.

## HEROES AND VILLAINS

Vikings loved tales of heroes and battles. In such tales, brave warriors behave well in battle or show courage fighting a fearsome monster. The old oral, or spoken, stories eventually passed into written poems such as the famous Anglo-Saxon poem *Beowulf*. This tells how a Danish warrior battles a man-eating monster Grendel. The poem was written in an early form of English, perhaps in the 700s, after the Anglo-Saxons had become Christians.

Beowulf has two adventures. In the first, he rescues his fellow Danes from Grendel, the evil monster that is carrying them off. In the second, he is now king and dies trying to protect his people from a fire-breathing dragon.

*Below:* In the Sigurd story, Gunnar was thrown into a snake pit. He made the snakes go to sleep by playing the harp with his toes. One snake did not sleep and it killed Gunnar. This carving is from a church doorway.

Some warrior tales recount real events. An Anglo-Saxon poem about the Battle of Maldon describes a fight in eastern England in 991 C.E. between the English and the invading Vikings. The poem tells how warriors behave, like Norse myth-heroes, fighting with honor to the last man and dying bravely.

Warriors put their trust in the gods and in magic. Most knew the story of Sigurd, whose adventures were told in myths in Scandinavia and Germany.

## LINK TO TODAY

Warrior-heroes are featured in stories such as *The Hobbit* and *The Lord of the Rings*. The human warrior, Boromir, is killed by Orcs as he protects the hobbit ring-bearer Frodo. In Norse myth, rings were often magical. Odin's ring, Draupnir, had the power of making new rings. This may have given author J. R. R. Tolkien the idea for the "ring of power" in *The Lord of the Rings*.

## THE LAST BATTLE

The Norse gods were destroyed in battle at Ragnarok, at the end of the world that brought the "twilight of the gods." From destruction, a new world was born. Ragnarok was foreshadowed by natural disasters: a three-year winter, earthquakes, the Sun darkened, raging monsters, and the giant ocean serpent causing waves to surge and overwhelm the world of men. Midgard froze, and all humans died but for one couple who took refuge in the World Tree, Yggdrasil.

### THE KING DEPARTS

The last battle theme recurs in other myths and stories such as the tales of King Arthur and the Knights of the Round Table. In the Arthur legend, of which there were many versions in the Middle Ages in Europe, Arthur is slain in battle with his enemies. The dead king is carried away in a ship, in a deathlike sleep, one day to return.

*Right:* In the legends of King Arthur, he and his brave knights battle against evil in a world of quests and magic. This French illustration dates from 1490.

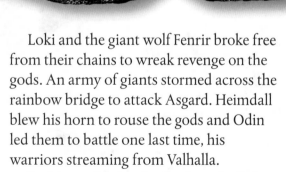

*Left:* The World Serpent makes an interesting subject for this Swedish brooch.

the wolf Fenrir. Loki and Heimdall killed each other. Thor battled the giant serpent Jormungand, slaying it only to die himself from its venom. Finally, Asgard itself was consumed by fire.

Then, from the ocean arose a new world, warmed by a new Sun. From the branches of Yggdrasil emerged the two survivors—the man and woman who would begin the world again. Baldur, god of light, was reborn and restored to rule alongside his blind brother Hoder, god of darkness. So in the end, the Norse myths provided hope for the future.

Loki and the giant wolf Fenrir broke free from their chains to wreak revenge on the gods. An army of giants stormed across the rainbow bridge to attack Asgard. Heimdall blew his horn to rouse the gods and Odin led them to battle one last time, his warriors streaming from Valhalla.

In this terrible battle, death took all the old gods. Odin was devoured in the jaws of

# NORSE LEGACY

**The Norse myths found their way into the literatures of Europe and beyond. Stories we enjoy today, and even some common words in English, can be traced back to the Norse peoples.**

Wherever they settled, the Norse took their beliefs, customs, and language. The English language is full of words from Old Norse and Anglo-Saxon, including words such as skin, skull, anger, knife, sky, and ship. Many customs of modern life have their roots in Norse and Germanic tradition, such as Yuletide at Christmas with decorated trees, burning logs, and mistletoe.

Though the old gods were rejected after Norse peoples became Christians, the old stories and myths were written down by the 1200s and became part of their national literatures, as sagas, epic poems, nursery rhymes, fairytales, novels, plays, and operas. Interest grew in the 1800s when, for example, the English writer William Morris wrote a poem about Sigurd, while the German composer Richard Wagner borrowed from Norse myth to create the series of four operas known as *The Ring of the Nibelungs*.

Viking visitors to North America did not settle long enough to leave evidence in map names. In Britain, however, place names ending in "by," such as Grimsby, suggest places where Vikings settled in the 800s and 900s. Other placename clues to Norse settlement are vik (bay), dal or dale (valley), sund (sound or strait), thorp (farm), and borg (town).

Archaeologists have uncovered secrets of the Norse world by excavating Viking settlements and burial sites. They have found boat graves such as the king's burial ship at Sutton Hoo, England. They have also found the remains of Viking ships, such as the Oseberg ship, now displayed in a museum in Norway.

## LINK TO TODAY

The English names for four of the days of the week come from Norse gods. Tuesday is "Tyr's day," Wednesday is "Woden's day," Thursday is "Thor's day," and Friday is "Frigg's day."

**Left:** The saga of Beowulf was originally a Norse story.
**Below:** The old Norse tale of Beowulf has been retold as a horror story in the movies.

EVIL BREEDS PAIN

BEOWULF

NOVEMBER

www.beowulfmovie.co.uk

## NORSE MYTHS IN MODERN CULTURE

Norse culture shaped the history of the Scandinavian nations, especially Norway, Denmark, and Sweden. By the 1200s C.E., the peoples of Scandinavia had abandoned their pagan religion for Christianity. They were among the last peoples of Europe to do so. The Anglo-Saxons and Germans had adopted Christianity much earlier. The old stories and beliefs survived in custom and literature and spread with European migrants to other lands, notably to the United States, to be preserved and retold in new ways.

*Below:* The thrash metal band Metallica are just one of many modern bands to have used Norse themes and images in their work.

### NORSE GOES POP

Norse myth imagery has influenced graphic design and pop music. Heavy metal bands in particular have chosen Norse myth imagery in song lyrics and album themes. Viking imagery can also be seen in some Goth-style and Hell's Angels' gear.

## THE MAGIC LIVES ON

Norse myths have had a wide influence on modern books, movies, and games. Writers and artists are attracted by the all-action tales and by the supernatural elements such as giants, dwarves, elves, dragons, and monsters. Magic is never far away in Norse myth, because the Norse religion was more about storytelling and magic than spiritual values, religious laws, or worship rituals.

Magic lies at the heart of many stories, which explains why modern culture has borrowed from Norse myth in books and movies. Some draw directly from the characters of the Norse gods, as in the movies *Thor* and *The Avengers*. Books such as J. R. R. Tolkien's *The Hobbit* and *The Lord of the Rings*, J. K. Rowling's *Harry Potter* series, and C. S. Lewis's *Narnia* books are all influenced by the Norse myth world.

Tolkien was a university teacher of medieval literature and set his stories in Middle Earth (Midgard), with magic rings, dwarves, dragons, wizards, monsters, and battles. Tolkien's books were so successful that today many fantasy novels feature Norse-myth characters.

*Below:* J. R. R. Tolkien's stories have been excitingly filmed as *The Lord of the Rings* and *The Hobbit* movie series.

## MODERN MYTHS

In Harry Potter's world, dragons guard the gold vaults in Gringott's goblin-run bank, house-elves are family servants, one of Harry's teachers is a werewolf, and among his enemies is another werewolf, Fenrir Greyback. There are science fiction novels in which Ragnarok is fought by Norse gods with modern weapons. More elements of Norse myth can be found in Terry Pratchett's *Discworld* books.

The superheroes of comics bear strong resemblances to Norse gods and heroes, some having the same names, such as Thor. They have supernatural powers—super-strong, can fly, see through walls, become invisible, change form, and so on—as they battle with monstrous foes. In Japan, artists have made comic strips and animated manga series about Ragnarok and Vinland, featuring characters named Freya, Valkyrie, and Odin.

The stories that were first told in the northlands of Europe more than 1,000 years ago continue to have a powerful and lasting effect.

**LINK TO TODAY**

Wars between gods, mortals, and giants are fertile sources for game creators. Norse myths live on in video/computer games, including *Tomb Raider: Underworld,* in which Lara Croft wields Thor's hammer. In the *Eve Online* game, spaceships have the names of gods and other characters from Norse myth, including Odin's ravens Hugin and Munin.

*Right:* Thor the god of thunder (far right) lives on today in video games (top right), and silver and gold jewelry based on his famous hammer (left) is popular.

# TIME CHART

**500 C.E** With the decline of the Roman Empire, Anglo-Saxons and other Germanic peoples migrate and settle in Britain, forming new "English" kingdoms

**600s** Swedish Vikings start to raid other countries

**625** King Raedwald buried with his ship and treasure at Sutton Hoo in England; the burial site was found in 1939

**793** Norwegian Vikings attack Lindisfarne monastery in England

**800s–1000s** Swedish Vikings travel across Russia to the Black Sea and Caspian Sea

**829** Christianity first reaches Sweden

**845** Vikings found Dublin in Ireland as a trading base

**865** Danish Viking armies invade England, fighting and eventually making peace with the English king Alfred the Great

**870** Vikings from Norway settle in Iceland

**911** Vikings control the region of northern France that becomes Normandy

**930** Vikings in Iceland set up the Althing, probably the world's first parliament

**985** Erik the Red from Norway leads a group of colonists to Greenland

**991** Battle at Maldon on the east coast of England as Viking invaders overwhelm the English defenders. The battle is later told in an Anglo-Saxon poem.

**1000** Leif Eriksson sails to North America, but Vikings do not settle there permanently

**1016** Danish Viking king Cnut rules as king of England, and also Norway and Denmark. Danish kings rule England until 1042.

**1066** William the Conqueror, a descendant of the Vikings, leads a Norman army to conquer England and end Anglo-Saxon rule

**1200** By this date, the *Poetic Edda* or *Elder Edda*, a collection of 38 poems about the Norse myths and beliefs

**1262** Iceland is ruled by the king of Norway

**1270** The *Prose Edda* or *Younger Edda* is written by Icelander Snorri Sturlusson

**1380** Norway and Denmark are united

**1800s** Interest in Norse myths grows among writers, artists, and musicians

**1814** Norway becomes part of Sweden

**1900s** Archaeologists discover numerous ship burials

**1905** Norway gains independence from Sweden

**1937** J. R. R. Tolkien's book *The Hobbit* is published

**2000s** Norse myths live on in movies, television shows, computer and video games, and books

# GLOSSARY

**Anglo-Saxons** People who lived in northern Germany

**archaeologists** People who study the past through digging up and examining ancient objects

**Asgard** Home of the Aesir gods

**chariot** A two-wheeled vehicle drawn by a horse or other animal

**commerce** Buying and selling goods

**dragon** Large mythical animal, often winged and often guards treasure

**dwarf** Small supernatural being, skillful smith and crafter, not always helpful to people in Norse stories

**elf** Supernatural being, usually helpful in Norse stories

**forge** To make objects from metal, such as swords and rings

**fjord** Narrow sea inlet between cliffs

**geyser** Spout of hot steam, water, and mud from underground

**isolated** Separate or cut off; remote

**longship** Viking ship with oars and a single square sail

**mead** Alcoholic drink made from honey and water

**migrant** Describes a person who travels to a new land to settle

**mortal** Will eventually die

**Odin** The ruler of the sky gods, or Aesir, and chief god in Norse myth

**outcast** Person who has been driven out from home or society

**pagan** Describes a religious belief in nature spirits and many gods, not one

**parliament** Supreme law-making council or assembly of a people or country

**phenomena** Remarkable or unusual events or happenings

**plumage** A bird's feathers

**propaganda** Influencing people by telling them what to think and do

**religion** A system of beliefs with prayers and offerings to gods, and worship in special buildings

**runes** Straight-line letters used as writing by Norse people, especially for memorials and magic spells

**sacrifice** An offering made to a god to seek the god's favor

**saga** Long stories of heroes and their adventures, first told aloud and later written down

**smith** Metalworker skilled at making tools and weapons

**supernatural** Out of this world; not of everyday natural experience

**troll** Supernatural being, like a giant, usually unpleasant

**underworld, the** A place where many people in ancient times believed the dead went

**Valhalla** The great hall in Asgard where Odin welcomed warriors killed in battle

# LEARNING MORE

## BOOKS

**Ashworth, Leon.** *Gods and Goddesses of Vikings and Northlands.* Mankato, MN: Smart Apple Media, 2003.

**Crossley-Holland, Kevin.** *The Penguin Book of Norse Myths: Gods of the Vikings.* New York: Penguin Books, 2011.

**D'Aulaire, Ingri, and Edgar Parin d'Aulaire.** *D'Aulaires' Book of Norse Myths.* New York: New York Review of Books, 2005.

**Denton, Shannon Eric, and Mateus Santolouco.** *Thor* (Short Tales, Norse Myths). North Mankato, MN: Magic Wagon, 2010.

**Heaney, Seamus.** *Beowulf* (translation). New York: W.W. Norton, 2000.

**Osborne, Mary Pope.** *Favorite Norse Myths.* New York: Scholastic, 2001.

## WEBSITES

The British Museum—Vikings
**www.britishmuseum.org/explore/cultures/europe/vikings.aspx**

BBC History—Vikings
**www.bbc.co.uk/history/ancient/vikings/**
**www.bbc.co.uk/schools/primaryhistory/vikings/**

Jorvik Viking Centre, UK
**www.jorvik-viking-centre.co.uk**

Nordic Heritage Museum, Seattle
**www.nordicmuseum.org/**

Viking Ship Museum, Norway
**www.khm.uio.no/vikingskipshuset/index_eng.html**

Vikings in Ireland—within the Archaeology section
**www.museum.ie/en/intro/archaeology-and-ethnography-museum.aspx**

Vikings in Canada
**www.canadianmysteries.ca/sites/vinland/home/indexen.html**

[Website addresses correct at time of printing.]

# INDEX

**A**egir  21, 26
Aesir gods  10, 13
Althing  25
Anglo-Saxons  4, 6
Arthur, King  38, 39
Asgard  10, 12, 13, 17, 19, 25,
    27

**B**aldur  13, 16, 17, 27
Beowulf  36, 41
berserkers  35
Brunhild  30, 36
burial ships  26–27, 33, 40

**c**hangelings  28
Christianity  19, 34, 40, 42
creation myths  8, 9

**d**ays of the week  40
dragons  14, 15, 36
dwarves  4, 15, 31

**e**arthquakes  22
elves  28, 31
English language  40
Eriksson, Leif  6, 27
Erik the Red  27

**f**amily life  29
farming  16, 29
Fenrir  19
festivals  31
forest trees  19

**F**reyja  12, 16, 28, 29
Freyr  16, 23, 33
Frigg  13, 17, 25

**G**erda  22, 23
geysers  8–9
giants  4, 8, 14
Ginnungagap  9

**H**eimdall  29
Hoder  17
horses  12, 32

**L**oki  12, 13, 15, 17, 19, 22, 27,
    33
longships  26, 33

**m**agic  14, 21, 30, 43
Midgard (Middle Earth)  9, 10,
    38, 43
Muspelheim  8, 9

**N**ine Worlds, the  6
Njord  27
Norns, the three  10, 19
Norse goddesses  13
Norse gods  11
Norse religion  4, 10, 19
Norse society  24, 29
Northern Lights  22, 23

**O**din  8, 10, 12, 13, 15, 17, 19,
    20, 24, 25

*Poetic Edda*  4
Potter, Harry  44, 45
*Prose Edda*  4

**R**agnarok  19, 29, 38
runes  17, 35

**s**ea, the  21, 26
Sif  33
Sigurd  15, 30, 36, 40
Skadi  27

**t**rade and commerce  32
treasure, buried  32
Thor  13, 20, 21 22
Tolkien, J. R. R.  37, 41
trolls  14
Tyr  19

**u**nderworld, the  10, 17, 19, 22

**V**alhalla  8, 10, 24, 35
Valkyries, the  22, 23, 30, 35
Vanir gods  13
Vikings, the  4, 35, 36, 37, 40

**w**arfare  34, 35
warriors  24, 34, 35, 36, 37
weapons  35
World Serpent, the  19, 20

**Y**ggdrasil  10, 18
Ymir  8, 9